The Gospel and Mental Illness

HEATH LAMBERT

CONTENTS

Part 1: Myths and Mental Illness in Biblical Counseling

1   Biblical Counselors Encourage Counselees to Quit   9
Taking Their Psychiatric Medication

2   Biblical Counselors Are Against Medical Science   13

3   Biblical Counselors Do Not Care About Suffering,
They Only Confront Sin   17

Part 2: The Spiritual Nature of Mental Illness

4   The Gospel and Mental Illness   23

5   Why Do We Ignore the Spiritual Nature
of Mental Illness?   27

6   Who Is Normal, Who Is Not, and A Biblical
Orientation of What Ails Troubled People   33

Part 3: Can Jesus Heal Mental Illness?

7   The Nature of Mental Illness   39

8   Mental Illness and the Healing of Jesus   43

9   The Importance of the Body   47

10   Mental Illness, Spiritual Issues, and Suffering   53

Part 1: Myths about Mental Illness in Biblical Counseling

1

BIBLICAL COUNSELORS ENCOURAGE COUNSELEES TO QUIT TAKING THEIR PSYCHIATRIC MEDICATION

One of the most persistent myths I hear about biblical counselors is that they are vehemently opposed to psychiatric medication and are trained to tell you to stop taking it. This is simply not true.

Taking psychiatric medications is controversial. Many people have legitimate questions about their use and effectiveness. Such questions and controversies are not unique to Christian conversations, either. Plenty of secular and medical professionals are writing book-length critiques of the use of psychoactive medications.

My job here is not to argue that the use of psychiatric medications is uncomplicated. Instead, my job is to state that the decision to use them is outside the professional purview of most counselors. Most people doing counseling today—of the biblical *or* secular variety—lack the medical licensing required to authorize the use of prescription medications. This means that most counselors lack the training and permission to be able to put people on or take people off of these medications.

Counselors may have opinions about such things. These opinions may even be well-informed, and backed-up with excellent scientific research. At the end of the day, however, they are just opinions. Any counselor who does not have a medical degree is simply not equipped, by law or professional training, to add behavior to their belief.

This same reality is true for most of the counselors certified by ACBC.

ACBC certifies many licensed and experienced medical doctors. Whenever we host an ACBC training event, one of these physicians is present to explain what we know and what we don't know about the use of psychoactive meds as well as other issues related to counseling and the physical body. One of the many things these physicians share with our counselors is that it is not their place to get people off their medications.

Many counselees desire to get off of their medication believing that they never really needed it, that it causes harmful side-effects, or that the biblical counseling they received removed the need for it. When counselees express a desire to come off their medication our medical doctors train counselors to send their counselee back to the physician who prescribed the medication for help with this. Several of our ACBC counselors with decades of medical experience will not take their own counselees off meds even though they possess a medical degree. Their reasoning: "I'm not the physician that put them on the medication, so I'm not going to be the physician to take them off."

The reason we teach our counselees to handle the issue of medication this way does not only have to do with their lack of a medical degree. The reasons also have to do with loving others well. When someone comes off these medications it can have a very serious effect on the body. A person's life can be threatened. These kinds of medical decisions where the health and safety of a human being are at stake must be left to medical professionals.

Does this mean that it has never happened that an ACBC counselor somewhere has told somebody to quit taking his medication? No, it doesn't mean that. I am confident that there is a cashier at the grocery store in your town who has stolen money from their register. When they steal the money, however, I don't think they do it because the manager told them to. I also don't think that if the manager found out about it that they would be awarded employee of the month.

I hope you can appreciate that the same is true at ACBC. If one of our counselors tells a counselee to come off of their medication they would be doing something we've told them not to do. They are working out of accord with their training, not in keeping with it. I also want you to know that when they do that, they are doing things for which they will be held accountable by our organization.

Physicians and researchers will be debating the utility of psychoactive meds for a long time to come. At the level of counseling practice, however, we know what the best practice is. We train our counselors that practical questions about the use of medication are best left to the physicians who can prescribe them.

Anybody that says anything else is just spreading a myth.

HEATH LAMBERT

2

BIBLCAL COUNSELORS ARE AGAINST MEDICAL SCIENCE

> "Biblical counselors don't think people have medical problems."

> "Biblical counselors think every problem is a spiritual problem."

> "Biblical counselors don't want anybody to go to the doctor they just think people need to get close to Jesus."

Every now and then you hear someone make a statement like one of these. You get the point: there is an idea floating around out there that biblical counselors don't like to talk about medical doctors, and don't like to use them because if people would only have a closer walk with Jesus then their life would be fine. The idea seems to be that if you're going to be committed to biblical counseling then there is no room for anything but spiritual problems.

This is just not true.

The Bible, Your Body, and Counseling Ministry

In fact, this is such a fabrication of what ACBC actually believes and teaches that it is hard for me to understand where it came from. Every single ACBC counselor I know goes to a physician when they are sick, and encourages their counselees to go see one when they need medical attention. It is our belief in the sufficiency of Scripture for counseling that encourages practices like that, rather than discouraging them.

As a matter of fact, the Bible—which we use as our authoritative and sufficient resource in counseling—drives us to embrace medical science. The Bible is clear that humans are embodied beings, rather than just spiritual ones. Because we are physical beings, the Bible encourages care for those physical bodies. Such teaching in Scripture invites the use of medicine, medical practitioners, and medical technology in caring for people.

Very personally, in my own counseling I am "trigger happy" on sending people to the doctor. My personal creed is *When in doubt, check it out.* When a counselee of mine is experiencing almost any kind of extreme in physical behavior I encourage a visit with a full physical. I believe such medical evaluations are part of counseling best practices. They constitute the "hearing a matter" that protects biblical counselors from folly and shame (Prov 18:13).

So Why the Myth?

If it is true that the Bible teaches the importance of care for your physical body, and if it is true that biblical counselors believe and practice the Bible . . . then why the myth?

Well, as I said before, I'm really not sure. Perhaps it is like the myths Arminians spread about Calvinists that they don't share the gospel. Maybe it is like the myths Calvinists spread about Arminians that they don't really trust God's sovereignty. It is all too easy to spread a caricature of someone's position instead of engaging the real thing.

If I had to take a crack at an explanation for the genesis of this particular myth, I'd suggest two realities.

Ministry Location

The first reality has to do with ministry location. Folks who are ACBC certified are trained to do ministry of the Word in the context of *counseling* ministry. We talk about problems in living from the perspective of life lived before a sovereign God. We point people with trouble to comfort from a Redeemer. We point people with sin to atonement from a crucified Christ. We point people overwhelmed with life's problems to a Christian community who can help bear their load. We are caring for people in this specific context.

We are not doing medical ministry. Medical ministry is important, and we are thrilled that there are many wonderful doctors available in our world today. The assumption that biblical counselors don't care about medicine because they don't practice medicine is as sane as assuming that surgeons don't care about sterile operating rooms because they're not on the cleaning crew.

Sometimes the best way to demonstrate that you're in favor of something is to leave it to those who know what they're doing.

The medical model vs. the moral model

A second reality driving this myth might be the medicalization of spiritual problems. As true as it is that people need medical attention for their physical problems, it is also true that we live in a secular culture that regularly attaches a medical diagnosis to problems that are actually moral and spiritual in nature.

We live in an increasingly secular culture that, in an effort to suppress the truth in unrighteousness, tries to redefine spiritual problems in terms of physical pathology. Scores of problems such as worry, sorrow over sin, and even teenage rebellion get mutated into secular diagnoses like anxiety disorder, dysthymic disorder, and obstinate defiant disorder.

When biblical counselors address these problems as the spiritual difficulties they are, we are not rejecting medical science. We're being the salt and light Jesus commanded all Christians to be. A society that tries to treat every spiritual problem with physical remedies is a secular one that has denied Christ and the Bible.

It is a myth that biblical counselors don't care about medical science. We care a great deal about it. We show that care in leaving the practice of medicine to those who know how to do it as a part of their vocational setting. We also show that care by refusing to prescribe physical remedies to spiritual problems that Jesus wants to heal.

3

BIBLICAL COUNSELORS DO NOT CARE ABOUT SUFFERING, THEY ONLY CONFRONT SIN

There is a great deal that many do not know about people certified by ACBC. One thing a lot of folks *think* they know, however, is that ACBC counselors disregard suffering, and only confront sin. This belief extends all the way back to the founding of the biblical counseling movement, and the ministry of Jay Adams. Adams has consistently been accused of dismissing the sorrows of his counselees in favor of an exclusive focus on sin.

Jay Adams and Compassionate Counseling

The works of Jay Adams were foundational and, like that of every other faithful Christian minister, in need of development and refinement. He initiated a model of counseling that was—by his own admission—incomplete, but still solid. The biblical counseling movement has been working hard to build on the solid foundation created by Adams. One of the areas where the biblical counseling movement has advanced is in the area of how to minister to folks who are suffering.

It is true that the biblical counseling movement has grown in the skill of teaching how to engage suffering people, but it is a myth that Jay Adams did not care about the sufferings of counselees. In fact, during a personal conversation with Dr. Adams several years ago I asked what was the most frustrating caricature that others repeat about him and his model of counseling. His response was moving. He said, "That I don't care about people who are hurting." He continued,

> For the life of me, I don't know how people came to think that I don't care about people who are in pain. People who accuse me of not caring don't see the letters I get from counselees who wrote thanking me that they are closer to the Lord because of the counseling we did together. They don't see the Christmas cards with pictures of families and notes on the back that say, "Thank you. These kids were born because God used your ministry to keep our marriage intact."

The founder of the biblical counseling movement was a man who cared about people enough to point them to a Savior who could comfort them in their weakness and cover their wickedness. It is love that led Jay Adams to connect struggling persons with a Redeemer.

How could a model motivated by such care be mythologized into something that is merely harsh and confrontational?

Nouthe-what?

I think a lot of it has to do with the term nouthetic. Adams made clear in the early pages of *Competent to Counsel* that the term, when translated from the Greek, was often rendered "admonish." Adams repeatedly connected the term with confrontation. Though this is a common translation of the term, Adams never intended it to have "harsh" connotations. In fact he said,

> *Nouthesis* is motivated by love and deep concern, in which clients are counseled and corrected by verbal means for their good, ultimately, of course,

that God may be glorified (Competent to Counsel, 50).

For Adams nouthetic confrontation was a loving extension of care from counselor to counselee. Unfortunately this understanding of nouthetic is not what stuck.

This situation is a little like the one of a family friend of mine who desperately wanted to be called "Nana" when her first grandchild was born. She would coo her new grandson and say, *Hi, sweetie, I'm Nana. Do you know your Nana, Sweetie? Sweetie, if you need anything you just tell your Nana.*

As soon as her grandson could speak he didn't begin calling her Nana. Instead he called her Sweetie. Now she is known to all of her grandchildren as Sweetie. The point—sometimes, despite our deepest desires and most strenuous efforts, our meaning can get lost.

I think something like that has happened with the word nouthetic and the caring intentions of the man who reintroduced the world to biblical counseling.

Biblical Counseling and Sin

I think another reason for the myth is that biblical counselors *do* address sin. We have to do that because the Bible insists upon it. We believe that sin is the problem that creates all counseling need, whether that sin is the personal sin of the counselee, the sin of the person victimizing the counselee, or the death and disease we experience because of the presence of sin in the world. We confront sin because we must confront sin to be effective counselors in a sinful world like this one.

Biblical counselors do not *only* confront sin, however. We care for people, counsel them free of charge, put our arm around them and cry with them when the pain is too intense to speak, we pray with them, encourage them, and teach them the Scriptures. We do all this and more.

Biblical counselors will be unique so long as they do something that other models avoid, namely, confront sin. Even though biblical counselors have other kinds of conversations, this may even be what stands out. It is a mythological claim, however, to say that those are the only conversations we have.

Part 2: The Spiritual Nature of Mental Illness

4

THE GOSPEL AND MENTAL ILLNESS

Is the Gospel about Mental Illness?

At ACBC we are committed to a specific kind of gospel ministry. We want to connect the most hurting and troubled people with the gospel of Jesus Christ in the context of counseling ministry. We certify counselors to minister the gospel of God's grace to all kinds of people whether they struggle with a mild spiritual problem, or the most serious mental health diagnoses.

The commitment makes many people wonder whether the Gospel has anything to do with mental illness. *Isn't mental illness a medical issue? How can the Gospel help with those kinds of things?* The temptation is to think that the Bible can't help with so-called mental issues because the one doesn't have anything to do with the other. For many it makes as much sense as having a biblical counseling commitment to car repair.

Is Mental Illness Spiritual?

In reality the Gospel has everything to do with mental illness. There are a number of ways I could demonstrate this, but for now let me tell you a story you may have heard. It is a story about a man named John Hinkley Jr.

Hinkley attempted to assassinate President Ronald Reagan

on March 30, 1981. Hinkley had become obsessed with actress Jodie Foster, and believed that if he could kill a president, he would be her equal and be able to get her attention. Hinkley opened fire on President Reagan at the conclusion of a speech and injured four people including the president, two law enforcement officers, and Reagan's press secretary.

In a very controversial verdict, Hinkley was found not guilty by reason of insanity. Over the years many different psychiatrists have debated what is wrong with Hinkley. He has had numerous diagnoses including depression, dysthymia, borderline personality disorder, schizophrenia, and schizoid personality disorder. Even more psychiatrists have debated whether Hinkley even has a mental illness. During the last three decades expert psychiatric testimony has conflicted over whether Hinkley should be institutionalized in a hospital or a penitentiary, and whether he should have increasing freedom.

Mad or Bad?

Such debates demonstrate that psychiatry doesn't provide the clarity of diagnosis and treatment we expect from many other scientific disciplines. The point I want to make here, however, is that even if we did conclude that Hinkley had something we might refer to as a "mental illness," wouldn't we also have to say that there is something fundamentally different from Hinkley than, say, a cancer patient? People with cancer, diabetes, and heart disease don't stalk women and open fire on a crowd in an attempt to murder a president. All disease exists in a world tainted by the sin of Adam, but there is something about many "mental illnesses" that are moral in a way that other diseases are not.

When you pay attention to the problems that our culture identifies as mental illnesses, you'll notice that they are often problems which involve an active human heart in ways that traditional diseases do not: folks diagnosed with clinical depression need hope and encouragement, folks labeled as alcoholics need to learn self-control, children identified with obstinate defiant disorder need to learn to respect their parents. What other diseases have hope, self-control, and submission as elements fundamental to cure?

What do the Mentally Ill Need?

Do not misunderstand me. I'm not trying to sit in judgment on all people diagnosed with a mental illness. I'm not comparing every person who has been diagnosed with a mental illness to John Hinkley. I'm also not saying that there is never anything medically wrong with people labeled with a psychiatric disorder.

What I *am* saying is that most mental illness diagnoses, spiritual issues of right and wrong, good and bad, obedience and disobedience are on the table in ways that they are not with traditional diseases. This means that people diagnosed with mental illness need the gospel in ways that are different than those with an actual disease.

I say "different" because all people need the gospel. The gospel is more important to a cancer patient than chemo; it is more important to a diabetic than insulin, it is more important to a heart patient than a bypass operation. The gospel provides the only solution that extends beyond a finite medical intervention to eternal life with Christ in heaven. The great need of every diseased person is the gospel of Jesus, even when the central treatment for their specific pathology is found outside the gospel.

This situation is not the case for those who carry the label of a mental illness. What pill can impart Christ-centered hope? What therapy can conjure up self-control? Has there ever been an ECT treatment that created submission? The answer to all of these questions is *no*. These realities are spiritual fruits that Jesus produces through his indwelling Spirit. This Spirit resides in those who believe the gospel.

Whatever we say about the biological and medical element of the various mental illnesses, we will say that no treatment for them is complete without a proclamation of the gospel, which alone brings the requisite changes in each of these problems.

This is why Christians need to have something to say about these issues. ACBC exists to help the church grow in wisdom about these issues, and to certify men and women who know how to bring the profundities of the gospel to the complexities of such difficult problems.

5

WHY DO WE IGNORE THE SPIRITUAL NATURE OF MENTAL ILLNESS?

Regardless of whatever biological factors are present in mental illness, most of those diagnoses will feature spiritual issues in ways that traditional diseases do not. This reality seems to be an obvious one whether the problem is a mild case of seasonal affective disorder or a more extreme diagnosis of dissociative identity disorder.

Merely Medical?

As true as this reality is many Christians overlook the spiritual essence of mental illness. One of the most significant reasons that Christians make this error has to do with an astonishingly secular assumption that an extreme problem is a medical problem.

When we observe people with problems that are debilitating, out-of-the-ordinary, scary, and hard to solve we can become disoriented in our evaluation. We have tended to adopt the prevailing secular understanding that extreme problems are biological problems.

There is no doubt that medical problems can often be extreme. We have disconnected from our biblical and God-centered worldview, however, when we ignore the

27

powerful and distorting effects of spiritual problems. In fact the most debilitating and scary problems in the cosmos stem from the spiritual problems we face.

Extreme Spiritual Problems

Consider a few examples of extreme spiritual problems . . .

King Saul, his kingship on the decline, vacillated between murderous spear-throwing, and strange displays of affection in his relationship with David. No amount of medical technology could ever diagnose a pathology in his body because there was nothing physically wrong with him. Saul's extreme problem was decidedly spiritual (1 Samuel 18-31)

When Job learned of the deaths of his children he engaged in a display of grief that must have been quite disturbing to see. Most of us would feel uncomfortable at Job's extreme reaction to his painful loss. He screamed at the top of his lungs, tore off his clothes, and shaved his head. I can imagine people in churches I've pastored saying privately—without intending to be mean—"I know this must be hard, but something is wrong with him. That just isn't normal. I wonder if he is sick?" In fact, Job was just fine physically, but, overwhelmed with grief, he behaved in an extreme way. (Job 1-2)

If the great Kingdom of Babylon existed in our day we would have a hard time processing the behavior of King Nebuchadnezzar. If the garden-variety Christian saw the mighty King flee from his palace to go live in the wild, act like an animal, and begin to eat grass he would know just what to do with him. He would commit him to a mental institution, expose him to a battery of tests, and put him in the orbit of the finest secular therapists money could buy. And none of it would work. Nebuchadnezzar was proud, and was being judged by God until he should humble himself. Nothing helped Nebuchadnezzar but a humble acknowledgement that the Lord was God (Daniel 4).

What would most people today think of a man running around in a graveyard, calling out, breaking chains, and cutting himself? Most would diagnose him with some sort of extreme mental illness, medicate him, and institutionalize him. When Jesus encountered such a man in the country of the Gerasenes, however, he did not recognize a man with a disease, but with a demon (Mark 5).

War of Worldview: Biblical Vs. Secular

These are just a handful of examples. The Bible is full of many more. The point is clear, however, that as Christians committed to a biblical worldview we must make room for the spiritual in our conception of extreme problems. Each of these problems, which today would easily earn an extreme diagnosis as a mental illness, is actually an extreme spiritual issue. None of these issues involved any expressly medical problem, but had to do with lying spirits from the Lord, desperate sorrow, divine judgment, and Satanic oppression.

To the secular, atheistic, humanistic, and postmodern conventions of psychiatry this must seem like mindless religious drivel. As Christians, though, we are convinced that these realities are the truth of God. Any Christian that cannot fold these situations (and many others) into their understanding of extreme problems is less-than-biblical in their understanding of what ails troubled people. We have forsaken our biblical and Christian heritage when we believe that the most extreme problems are medical, rather than spiritual in nature.

Not Simplistic, But Complex

Folks operating from a biblical worldview get accused of being simplistic, but actually it is secular people who are open to this charge. What is simplistic is to assume that all extreme problems can only have their genesis in medical problems. What is more nuanced and complex is a dynamic and sophisticated model that allows for the intersection of spiritual and biological factors in the extreme problems of mental illness. Only the approach of biblical counseling can offer this kind of multi-dimensional approach.

The Bible is pretty clear that tons of extreme problems are essentially spiritual problems. This should motivate Christians to avoid forsaking the area of "mental illness" as one about which we have nothing to say. Instead we should move towards the most troubled people in our society with spiritual solutions that will be full of power when the best medical interventions are irrelevant.

6

WHO IS NORMAL, WHO IS NOT, AND A BIBLICAL ORIENTATION OF WHAT AILS TROUBLED PEOPLE

What is Wrong with the Mentally Ill?

What is wrong with people diagnosed as mentally ill? What state of pathology or lack of health earns the label *illness*? Psychiatry does not render a diagnosis of illness the way other medical practitioners do. There is no blood test for "clinical depression," no biopsy detects bipolar disorder, a CT scan cannot identify borderline personality disorder.

A diagnosis of mental illness is not usually a medical diagnosis at all. It is an evaluation of behavior based off a subjective standard of what actions and attitudes are considered to be normal or abnormal. People are considered mentally ill when they think, feel, and do things outside the range of what normal people do.

Normality and Abnormality

In his book, *Saving Normal*, Dr. Allen Frances has an interesting discussion about what makes someone normal and what makes someone abnormal. Dr. Frances is the former chairman of the department of psychiatry at Duke University and served as the chairman of *The Diagnostic and Statistical Manual of Mental Disorders IV (DSM-IV)*. Writing as a leading psychiatrist with decades of experience in his field, Dr. Frances is concerned about the sliding scale of normalcy, psychiatry's institutionalization of which behaviors are normal and which ones are not, and the assignment of "mental illness" to those who are different.

Frances spends an entire chapter of his book explaining just how challenging it is to define normal. Then he describes, from his experiences leading DSM-IV, how hard it is to define mental illness and abnormality. On page 16 of his book he writes:

> I have reviewed dozens of definitions of mental disorder (and have written one myself in DSM-IV) and find none of them the slightest bit helpful either in determining which conditions should be considered mental disorders and which not, or in deciding who is sick and who is not.

This is a stunning admission from one of the world's foremost psychiatrists and the leader of the most influential guidebook on mental illness in the world. Frances believes that our efforts at defining mental illness, normality, and abnormality are not the slightest bit helpful in determining who is sick and who is not.

Is Normal the Standard?

Though he is a significant leader, Frances' statement is controversial. There are doubtless many other psychiatrists who would disagree with him. Fine. But Frances got me thinking: What is normal? Is normal a biblical standard for what ails troubled people?

In fact it is not. When you read the Bible you discover that what is normal or typical—what surrounds the mean—is not the standard. Lying is normal, but it isn't legitimate. Faithless sex is ordinary, but it is no benchmark. Pride is as commonplace as the air, and yet is a terrible standard. All sorts of things are normal, and yet terrible.

The Bible's standard isn't normalcy. It is righteousness. Listen to the Apostle Paul:

> For the sake of Christ I have suffered the loss of all things and count them as rubbish, in order that I may gain Christ and be found in him, not having a righteousness of my own that comes from the law, but that which comes through faith in Christ, the righteousness from God that depends on faith (Philippians 3:8-9).

Paul's driving passion is not to become normal. It is to be found in Christ and his righteousness.

One of the reasons psychiatrists argue so much about what is wrong with troubled people is that they are measuring against the wrong standard of normalcy. The Bible calls us to the righteousness of Christ. People's problems do not concern any problem with abnormality. We are all born sinners and continue in that state apart from grace. People aren't messed up because they are abnormal. They are messed up because they are wrong. Sin is the defining standard of normalcy for all of us.

This means that the most significant problem people face is that they are far too normal. What people need is not more normalcy, but more righteousness. The Bible teaches that this righteousness comes by faith. It is in understanding this that you will come to know that the most troubled people among us need the gospel, embraced by faith, far more than they need to be normal.

Part 3: Can Jesus Heal Mental Illness?

7

THE NATURE OF MENTAL ILLNESS

One of the questions we get asked a lot in the biblical counseling movement concerns whether Jesus can heal those with a mental illness. The question is asked by people who are concerned about Scripture's sufficiency and Jesus' relevance to deal with the most difficult problems that people face. Before we can answer the question we need to know what we are talking about. That means we need to know what mental illness is.

Defining Mental Illness

Defining mental illness is harder to do than you might imagine. That is because psychologists don't really know what it is. There are scores of books on my shelves full of secularly trained professionals debating what mental illness is and whether it exists. Interestingly, even the writers of psychology's authoritative manual on mental illness, *The Diagnostic and Statistical Manual of Mental Disorders (DSM)*, cannot agree on what constitutes a mental illness.

There has been a lot of attention in the psychology community over the fact that the most recent edition of the manual, DSM-V, made a substantial change to the definition of mental illness included in its previous edition, DSM-IV. They made this definitional change without explanation, and without presenting any evidence concerning why it needed to be changed.

Writing in *Psychology Today*, psychologist Dr. Eric Maisel points out in fascinating language the difficulty of being able to change a definition so easily.

> *The very idea that you can radically change the definition of something without anything in the real world changing and with no new increases in knowledge or understanding is remarkable, remarkable until you realize that the thing being defined does not exist. It is completely easy— effortless, really—to change the definition of something that does not exist to suit your current purposes. In fact, there is hardly any better proof of the non-existence of a non-existing thing than that you can define it one way today, another way tomorrow, and a third way on Sunday.*

For Maisel, a secular psychologist, the definition of mental illness can be changed so easily because mental illness does not really exist.

So, What is Mental Illness?

Mental illness is not a disease in the way that tuberculosis or hepatitis is. Mental illness is more in the realm of what social scientists call a construct. A construct is not an object like a tractor or table. It is an idea like beauty or relevance. A construct is a relatively abstract idea that gets informed by the shifting opinions of various people. Mental illness is a construct. Psychologists Herb Kutchins and Stuart Kirk have each served on the DSM committees, whose votes decide what is and is not a mental illness. They say,

The category of [mental illness] itself is an invention, a creation. It may be a good and useful invention, or it may be a confusing one. DSM is a compendium of constructs. And like a large and popular mutual fund, DSM's holdings are constantly changing as the managers' estimates and beliefs about the value of those holdings change.

Mental illness is a shifting idea that different people fill up with different categories at different times. For the most part it is a category that gets used by secular psychologists to describe behaviors that are outside the range of normal. I have described in chapter six that for Christians our standard is not normalcy, but righteousness.

Mental Illness and Worldview

Before we can answer whether Jesus can heal mental illness, we need to be sure we know what we are talking about. Understanding that mental illness is a construct means that Believers have a responsibility to fill up that category with their biblical worldview, rather than a secular one.

Psychology informs the construct of mental illness with a secular, materialistic worldview. They do not believe that people are spiritual beings who live all of their life under the authority of a God who made them and holds them accountable. Denying the Divine and the spiritual requires them to see all problems as physical and organic in nature. Worry isn't sinful; it is an organic mental illness that requires medical intervention. Sorrow isn't spiritual; it is a medical problem that requires a pharmacological solution.

As Christians we know better.

Jesus teaches that these problems—and thousands more like them—are spiritual problems that grow out of the heart of man (Mark 7:14-23). Certainly they impact the body, and the body can have its own problems as well. But the assigning of spiritual problems like anger, worry, and sorrow to the medical realm is unbiblical, unchristian, and a rejection of the clear statements of Jesus about the problems people have.

Mental Illness and Jesus

Mental illness is a label secular thinkers assign to spiritual problems discussed in the Scriptures. In the next chapter I'll talk about what Jesus and his healing have to do with all of this.

8

MENTAL ILLNESS AND THE HEALING OF JESUS

"Mental Illnesses" and Spiritual Issues

In the previous chapter I tried to demonstrate that mental illness is not a concrete object like a wheelbarrow, but is an abstract idea like friendship. A concrete object is what it is. An abstract idea is open to interpretation and definition by the worldview commitments of the person describing the idea. Secular psychologists have a terrible time defining mental illness, but usually relate it to behavior that is unusual and suggest some kind of medical intervention to deal with it.

Christians need to understand that many mental illnesses are actually spiritual issues. If this is the case then we need to ask whether Jesus can bring healing to these things.

The Bible, Healing, and Spiritual Issues

The question is important because we often think of healing with respect to physical issues like a broken bone or Lou Gehrig's disease. On the other hand, the Bible does not limit healing to physical issues. Scripture talks about healing with respect to spiritual matters as well.

The LORD builds up Jerusalem; he gathers the outcasts

of Israel. He heals the brokenhearted and binds up their wounds. (Psalm 147:2-3)

There is one whose rash words are like sword thrusts, but the tongue of the wise brings healing. (Proverbs 12:18)

Make the heart of this people dull, and their ears heavy, and blind their eyes; lest they see with their eyes, and hear with their ears, and understand with their hearts, and turn and be healed. (Isaiah 6:10)

These are a few examples. There are many more (Pss 30:1-3, 107:19-20; Prov 13:17, 29:1; Isa 53:5, 57:18; Jer 15:18; Hos 6:1—and more!). God is actually rather fond of using healing language in a poetic way to refer to God's restoration of our sins and sufferings.

Healing Language in a Mental Illness Culture

On the authority of Scripture Believers can talk about Jesus healing spiritual issues that our culture often calls mental illness. But this makes some people nervous. They think if we use the language of healing for mental illnesses we give credence to a secular view that sees spiritual problems as physical in nature.

I understand that concern, and actually share it. In fact, I used to avoid the language of healing with regard to spiritual issues for the same reason. Then I grew in my understanding of the authority and sufficiency of Scripture. The authority and sufficiency of Scripture means that we must not allow secular psychology to have the role of determining how we speak about the counseling problems people face or their solutions. God gets to decide how we refer to the issues people face in their lives, not psychology. If we refuse ever to use the language of healing for spiritual matters, we're guilty of the same kind of rejection of the sufficiency of Scripture as those who insist on referring to teenage rebellion as obstinate defiant disorder. Neither person is using God's language to describe problems and solutions.

Healing in Christ Alone

When it comes to mental illness the professionals disagree on a definition, and most laypeople really have no idea what they're talking about. If Christians are going to use the language to engage unbelievers and uninformed Christians in a conversation, we need to carefully explain that mental illness is secular language for problems that usually have to do with life lived before the God of heaven and earth. We need to further explain that it is Jesus alone who can deal with these problems.

Jesus really can heal these problems. In fact, his is the only healing available. Our culture believes that mental illnesses point to biology and require medical intervention. Those of us in the biblical counseling movement are the only ones who know that the construct of mental illness actually has to do with problems of the heart and require the gospel of God's grace for healing.

It is we biblical counselors who understand that secular psychology *heals the wounds of God's people lightly* (Jeremiah 6:14). In a culture of mental illness we must be the people who point to Jesus who *bore our sins in his body on the tree, that we might die to sin and live to righteousness. By his wounds you have been healed* (1 Peter 2:24).

9

THE IMPORTANCE OF THE BODY

Jesus, Healing, and the Spiritual Nature of Mental Illness

In chapter seven I discussed the difficulty of defining mental illness because it is not a concrete object, but an abstract idea that is open to interpretation by many different people. I suggested that Believers must understand many mental illnesses as spiritual issues.

In chapter 8, I showed from the Scriptures that it is appropriate to talk about healing these issues since the Bible discusses healing in both organic and spiritual terms.

Jesus not only can heal these spiritual issues, but in fact provides the only healing available.

But when we underline the spirituality behind mental illness it raises a very important question that biblical counselors better be able to answer. What is the relationship of physical issues to mental illness? We must answer whether the body has any role to play in these matters, and how Jesus' healing is relevant for them.

In Scripture, the Body is Honored

The Bible is clear that God made human beings to consist

of a body and a soul.

> *The LORD God formed the man of the dust from the ground and breathed into his nostrils the breath of life, and the man became a living creature (Gen 2:7).*

Every individual is a tight union of two constituent parts. Each person is one human being composed of both a physical and a spiritual essence. We make distinctions between these two constituent parts carefully understanding that they are only divisible at death, and—even at that—will ultimately be restored together on the Last Day.

Throughout Church history some have wanted to dishonor the body by devaluing it, but the Bible will not allow such an approach.

> *Do you not know that your bodies are members of Christ? . . . Do you not know that your body is a temple of the Holy Spirit within you, whom you have from God? (1 Cor 6:15, 19)*

We could never imagine a more exalted status for our bodies than that they would be considered members of Jesus Christ himself and the dwelling place of God the Holy Spirit. The Bible's emphasis on the importance of our bodies means that we must love, honor, and care for them. We can do this in any number of ways. In the context of 1 Corinthians 6 we do this by pursuing sexual purity. First Timothy 4:8 makes clear that we can accomplish this with physical exercise, which is of some value.

In the context of illness and disease we love, honor, and care for our bodies by embracing medical care for medical problems. This means that any counselor worth his salt should enthusiastically embrace the use of physicians, medicines, surgeries, and other procedures for cure and symptom relief. We are in favor of everything from a soothing cup of tea while nursing a head cold, to deep brain surgery for Parkinson's patients, and everything in between.

The Bible's teaching on the nature of who we are as humans with a body and a soul is a great help in counseling. When we think of counselees as whole persons we will always want to be aware of both physical and spiritual issues as we care for people.

Paying attention to both helps us to avoid two equal and opposite errors. On one hand is the error of the prosperity gospel, which sees nefarious spiritual problems at the root of every physical difficulty. On the other hand is the error of secular psychology with its materialistic view of mankind that ignores any spiritual problems in favor of an exclusive focus on physicality.

"Mental Illness" is Confusing

Secular psychologists have an unbiblical view of persons as merely physical. Because of this their efforts at classifying problems in *The Diagnostic and Statistical Manual of Mental Disorders (DSM)* runs afoul. The book is confusing. Lacking the clarity and truthfulness of the Bible it is not able to make scriptural distinctions between physical and spiritual issues. This requires Christians reading it to exercise great discernment.

The DSM lists hundreds of disorders under the category of illness. Disorders like Autism Spectrum Disorder, Seasonal Affective Disorder, Bipolar I, Bipolar II, Disruptive Mood Dysregulation Disorder, and Schizpoid Personality Disorder are all placed together in the same status of mental illness. Some of these hundreds of disorders, like Autism, are obviously physical in nature. Others, like Disruptive Mood Dysregulation Disorder, have no supporting evidence for any physical component at all. A person reading the DSM has no way to tell from within the manual which problems have a medical and organic basis, and which ones do not.

The DSM lumps spiritual issues, physical issues, and combinations of the two all into the category of illness. A Christian view of personality forces us to think more clearly than this. We need to connect the spiritual problems of people to the spiritual solutions found in Christ and his Word. We need to connect the physical problems of people to the solutions offered by competent medical professionals. Often, we need to do both of these at once.

Being Careful

The biblical teaching that humans have a body and soul is a great help to us in ministering to troubled people, but we need to be careful. The intersection of body and soul is somewhat mysterious and it can often be hard to tell whether problems belong in one category, another category, or some combination of the two.

I think Ed Welch is very helpful on this topic in his book *Blame it On the Brain*. Welch argues that spiritual issues will show up as moral categories that the Bible endorses or condemns. Physical issues show up as amoral categories that the Bible doesn't pronounce an ethical verdict on (i.e., the forgetfulness of Alzheimer's disease is never indicted in Scripture and so we know it is a physical weakness that requires physical care).

As helpful as these distinctions are we still must be cautious. Whenever problems appear extreme, out of the ordinary, or potentially biological in any way I refer my counselees to a physician. Receiving a full medical work-up allows us to rule out organic issues or else ensure that people with physical problems get the medical treatment they require.

Jesus' Healing and Physical Issues

So, after all this we still must answer the question about Jesus' healing when physical issues are on the line. Does all this mean Jesus doesn't heal when the issues are physical in nature? My answer is no for several reasons.

First, when people are plagued with physical problems it is Jesus—in his common grace—that makes available all the medical knowledge and help currently available to us. When medical treatments work we should express gratitude to physicians and drug manufacturers. Ultimately, however, we must give praise to God who is the giver of every good gift.

Second, Jesus can and does intervene when modern

medicine cannot and heals miraculously. We should boldly ask Jesus to heal us, understanding that though he can heal he also often loves to use persistent illness to grow our trust in him through our own weakness.

Third, When people are plagued with physical problems it is Jesus who draws near to them comforting them and empowering them to endure their diagnosis. Patients need Jesus to be near to them and minister tender mercy whether their prognosis is positive or negative. The most significant issues in life do not have to do with medicine but with life lived before the face of a good and sovereign God. It does not demean the body to confess that people always need spiritual healing more than the physical variety

Fourth, when people are plagued with physical problems the most successful medical relief they receive is only temporary. Every medical treatment—no matter how wonderful—will ultimately fail when our bodies succumb to the final enemy, death. On the day our spirit is torn from our body we will need to look to Jesus to provide for us what no medical doctor ever can. We will need our Savior himself and the hope he offers of a glorified body, cleansed from weakness, that will never again know death, mourning, crying, or pain.

On the Last Day the only medical intervention that will matter is the one from the Great Physician. He will show us then that he honors our bodies more than we ever could. We need to long for that day when we are with him. Until then, we honor him, the Bible, our bodies, and sick people by going to human doctors who require a co-pay.

10

MENTAL ILLNESS, SPIRITUAL ISSUES, AND SUFFERING

Before concluding, I want to talk about the relationship of suffering to the spiritual issues that our culture often refers to as mental illness. At times the biblical counseling movement has received a bad rap for equating the kinds of spiritual issues on the table in counseling with sin. I want to make clear that sins aren't the only kinds of spiritual issues that biblical counselors want to address.

Sin is an Issue in Counseling

Many people that come for help are struggling with sinful living. Rage, lust, anxiety, and selfishness are all problems psychology medicalizes. God calls them sin. Christians committed to counseling the Scriptures are literally the only people who know this, who can call these problems what they are, and offer true help.

Many people are concerned that Christians who point out sin to their counselees will make them feel guilty. Such thoughts are misplaced. Sinful people *are* guilty whether they feel it or not. In Christ we have a redeemer who rescues us from the guilt of sin. When biblical counselors point out sin they are pointing out a difficulty for which we have a solution in the person and work of

Jesus. Secular psychologists call this guilt inducement. The Bible calls it good news!

People Suffer Too

Though sin is an issue in biblical counseling, it is not the only one. People come to counseling for many reasons that extend beyond their own personal sin. Spouses are victims of domestic violence, children are molested by those they love, people are in spiritual turmoil over a devastating medical diagnosis. There are hundreds and thousands of reasons why someone might seek counseling help for a difficulty that is not their fault.

Depression is one example.

In The Sermon on the Mount Jesus says, *He opened his mouth and taught them, saying: Blessed are the poor in spirit, for theirs is the kingdom of heaven (Matt 5:2-3).*

In this passage Jesus talks about those who are poor in spirit. Different people in different cultures use different language to refer to people called poor in spirit. Whether we call it melancholy, sorrow, anguish, or depression there is a category of sad people who are not judged by Jesus, but honored and promised reward. The people who are sad in the way Jesus discusses here are not condemned, but esteemed.

The kind of sorrow that Jesus is referencing here is anguish over sin, but the sorrow itself is praiseworthy. Only a faithless counselor would rebuke a person in such pain. Jesus, the wonderful counselor, promises them the Kingdom!

Multiple Kinds of Sorrow

The Apostle Paul talks about two kinds of sorrow in 2 Corinthians 7. There is worldly sorrow that leads to death and godly sorrow that leads to life (2 Cor 7:10). The worldly sorrow that leads to death is sorrow, which is focused on self and the things of the world, rather than God. The godly sorrow that leads to life is focused on Jesus. Worldly sorrow is bad, and needs a rebuke. Godly sorrow is virtuous, and worthy of praise.

The biblical teaching in this regard is helpful in several ways.

First, it keeps us from the error of thinking that it is never wrong to be sad. There is a kind of anguish that the Bible condemns.

Second, however, it keeps us from the error that all sorrow is bad and needs correcting. The kind of sorrow Paul emphasizes with the Corinthians is *good* sorrow. Paul was happy that the Corinthians had this kind of anguish (2 Cor 7:9). There is a certain kind of sorrow we should encourage.

When you understand the importance of the body as we discussed in Part 3 of this series we also can make room for sorrow that is not spiritual, as in 2 Corinthians 7, but is physical. For example if a person has a problem called hypothyroidism their thyroid does not produce enough thyroid hormone. This will lead to feelings of intense sorrow. This is not the fault of the person with the problem. They have a physical weakness for which they need medical help. When we draw near to such people with that kind of care the Bible calls it helping the weak (1 Thess 5:14).

Counseling and Comfort

Biblical counselors should want to provide ultimate comfort to any who come for counseling. We must understand that people who are struggling with sins are suffering in ways they might not even appreciate. Providing ultimate comfort to them means extending a loving, gentle rebuke.

We should also want to comfort folks who are struggling with pain that doesn't need a rebuke. In this brief discussion on depression we looked at three causes for it in the Bible and saw that two are spiritual in nature, and one is physical. Only one kind of sorrow needs a rebuke-- that is the spiritual variety that has to do with sin. The other two kinds of sorrow, suffering and physical issues, require encouragement and physical care.

This is biblical evidence that requires all of us to move towards people offering help with their sufferings, not merely their sin. It is also strong encouragement in the varied and profound wisdom provided in the Scriptures. There is no source in the world, outside the Bible, that supplies such wisdom

ABOUT THE AUTHOR

Heath Lambert serves as the Executive Director of the Association of Certified Biblical Counselors (ACBC), a biblical counseling organization with certified members in 18 countries. He is also the associate professor of biblical counseling at The Southern Baptist Theological Seminary and their undergraduate institution, Boyce College.

Dr. Lambert is the author of *The Biblical Counseling Movement After Adams* (Crossway), *Finally Free: Fighting for Purity with the Power of Grace* (Zondervan), and the editor (with Stuart Scott) of *Counseling the Hard Cases: True Stories Illustrating the Sufficiency of God's Resources in Scripture* (B&H)

He is honored to live with his four favorite people in the world: his wife, Lauren, and their three children, Carson, Chloe, and Connor.

Made in the USA
San Bernardino, CA
28 December 2018